Tree ID Made Easier

A full color photo guide plus helpful hints for identifying
major trees of the Southern U.S.

by
Dan D. Williams

Possum Publications
Athens, Georgia

<u>**Primary Reference For This Book:**</u>

<u>**Guide to Southern Trees**</u>

by
Ellwood S. Harrar
and
J. George Harrar.

Dover Publications, 1962

This book is cordially dedicated to my wife, best friend and camping buddy, Jenny

All photographs, unless otherwise noted are by Dan Williams.

TABLE OF CONTENTS

INTRODUCTION

This book is for beginners; folks who want to learn to identify trees, but are possibly daunted by detailed and comprehensive manuals. This book can not replace those manuals. Instead, it provides a fast-track introduction to tree id that enables the reader to quickly grasp the subject, and better understand the more complex guides.

In Chapter 1., the reader learns three important but easy tree tips for identifying trees based on leaf arrangement characteristics:

simple leaves versus compound leaves

opposite leaves versus alternate leaves

leaf lobes versus leaf teeth

Major Southern trees are placed in one of six groups based on the above tree tips. A mnemonic (memory helper) for remembering the trees in each group is provided. This technique lets you quickly tell which group a tree belongs to, and gives you an easy way to remember the trees in the group. Once you know the tree's group, refer to the one-liner descriptions and color photographs to help you decide which tree is your tree.

There are many good tree identification guides available for more detailed and comprehensive information about Southern trees. Native Trees of the Southeast ,by L. Kathryn Kirkman, Claud L. Brown and Donald J. Leopold is one we recommend as an overall guide. A field Guide to the Trees and Shrubs of the Southern Appalachians, by R. E. Swanson, is a good guide that focuses on Southern mountain trees and shrubs.

The memory mnemonics in this book are both ridiculous and useful! Even an experienced dendrology (tree id) professor would have trouble naming the major trees in just one of the six tree groups without some kind of memory aid. Once you learn these silly sayings, you'll be able to rattle off the major trees in all six groups, a useful tool for tree identification as well as verbal and written communication.

HELPFUL INFORMATION

Blue Squares: The blue squares on each tree photo are one inch on a side. They show you how big or small the leaf is.

Canopy, Subcanopy and Understory Trees: Canopy trees, like oaks are the tallest trees in the forest. They form the forest roof or canopy. Subcanopy trees, like sourwood grow just below the canopy. Understory trees, like dogwood are small and grow in the understory.

Fruit: This word is used to mean what ever kind of "seed-holding" body the tree produces. It could be a berry, a capsule or a cone.

Fruit Ripeness: Some of the photos show unripe tree fruit structures, while others show ripe fruit. Keep in mind that you may see fruit on a tree that looks a little different from the photos in this book. As they ripen, tree fruits usually go through several shapes and colors.

Fuzzy versus hairy: Fuzzy and hairy mean the same thing in this book. They just mean, there is something there you can feel or see.

Size: Here is what we mean:

      short or small----shorter than a computer mouse

      medium-----wide as a computer keyboard
                    front-to-back

      long or tall-------long as a computer keyboard

CHAPTER 1. THREE TREE TIPS

Tip 1. Simple versus compound leaves

Tree leaves may be either simple or compound. **Simple** leaves are made of a single structure (a leaf) attached to a <u>woody or semi-woody</u> twig. **Compound** leaves are made of many identical leaflets attached to a (usually) <u>flexible green</u> leaf stem. Leaflets are almost always eye-shaped (elliptical).

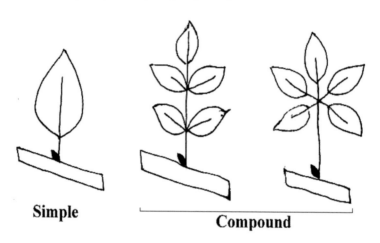

Simple   **Compound**

How to tell a leaf from a leaflet
Grab the possible leaf. Follow it back to where it attaches to the tree. If it attaches to a <u>slender green flexible</u> stem, then it is a leaflet. It will most likely be roughly eye-shaped, and one of many identical leaflets arranged opposite each other on the green flexible leaf stem.

If the possible leaf attaches to a <u>woody or semi-woody</u> stem, then it really is a leaf. Simple leaves can have many shapes, including eye-shape.

Another clue to recognizing a leaf is its axillary bud. This is a bud situated at the base of the leaf where it attaches to the twig. If you find this bud, you know you have a leaf. Axillary buds can be confusing, though, because they are not always visible.

Some trees like ashes and hickories have swollen leaf bases, but most don't, so use this as a clue along with other information.

Tip 2. opposite versus alternate leaves

The leaves of all trees are arranged in one of two ways. **Opposite** leaves attach to the twig opposite each other. **Alternate** leaves attach to the twig one above the other (alternately). The drawing below illustrates the two arrangements. A tree's twigs and branches are also arranged in this way, a very helpful winter id tool.

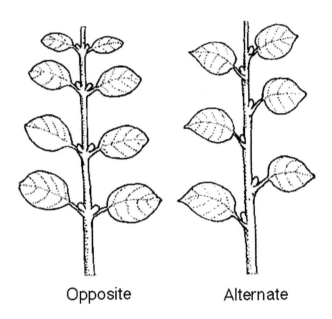

Opposite   Alternate

BEWARE! Leaflets on a compound leaf are almost always attached **opposite** each other on the flexible green leaf stem, but this does not mean the leaves are opposite.

First determine what one leaf looks like, then decide if the leaves are opposite or alternate.

Tip 3. lobes and teeth

Some trees like oaks have **lobed** leaves. Lobes are large, usually rounded leaf projections separated by indentions. Other trees like dogwood have **unlobed** leaves.

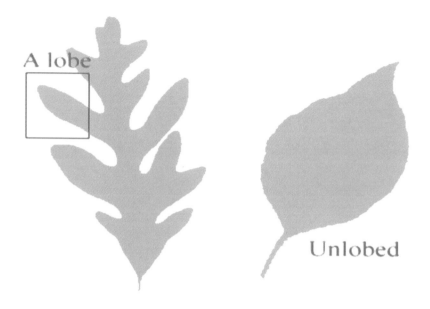

A lobe

Unlobed

Some trees like elms have **toothed** leaves with teeth located along the the leaf edge. Others like persimmon have **toothless** leaves.

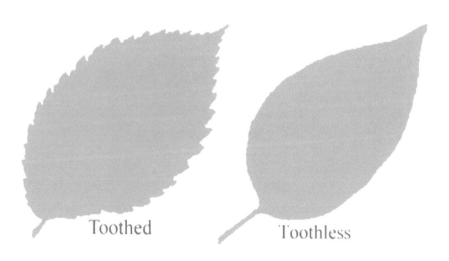

Toothed

Toothless

CHAPTER 2. HOW TO IDENTIFY A TREE

Most folks can tell a conifer tree like pine or cedar from a "broadleaf" tree, like maple or oak. If your tree is a <u>conifer</u>, go to Chapter 8 (page 60).

For a broadleaf tree, first determine what one leaf looks like (page 6), then decide whether the tree has simple or compound leaves.

Second, determine if the leaves are opposite or alternate. Remember not to confuse a leaflet with a leaf during this process.

Now check to see if the leaves are lobed or unlobed.

Finally, check for toothed versus untoothed leaves.

Congratulations, you now have the information necessary to find your tree's group. Here is a list of the tree groups:

CHAPTER 3. TREES WITH COMPOUND LEAVES

"Hicks Peeking over a Low Wall at a Box of Ashes"

Hickory, **P**ecan, **B**lack **L**ocust, **H**oney**L**ocust, **W**alnut, **B**oxelder, **A**sh

Pignut Hickory _(Carya glabra)_

5 leaflets per leaf.
nuts are pear shaped (have a pig nose)
outer black husk does not split completely open after falling
twigs slender and hairless
bark often flaky compared to other hickories

Sand Hickory (_Carya pallida_), not pictured here has 7 small leaflets per leaf. The leaf underside and twig buds are covered with very small yellowish dots (use a hand lense) . This tree grows on dry rocky sites, like those underlain by sandstone.

Red Hickory *(Carya ovalis)*

5 and 7 leaflets per leaf.
nuts are round in shape
black husk does split, releasing the tan nut.
husks are thinner than those of mockernut
twigs slender and hairless

Mockernut Hickory *(Carya tomentosa)*

7 and 9 leaflets per leaf.
twigs and buds are thick and fuzzy
crushed leaves and twigs have a strong odor
black husks are thick, & split releasing a large tan nut
bark usually deeply ridged, not flaky

Bitternut Hickory *(Carya cordiformis)*

grows almost exclusively in <u>stream bottoms</u>.

<u>7, 9 and 11 leaflets</u> per leaf.

twig end buds are made of <u>two sulfur yellow bud scales</u>

bark often marked with <u>whitish patches</u>

Pecan *(Carya illinoensis)*

9 to 17 leaflets per leaf

leaflets are <u>sickle shaped (curved)</u>

terminal leaflet (the one on the leaf end) usually <u>present</u>

nut is the familiar pecan

widely planted as a commercial nut crop

Black Locust *(Robinia pseudoacacia)*

  restricted to the <u>Mountains</u> and upper Piedmont
  leaflets are oval shaped
  has <u>thorns that look like large rose thorns</u>
  fruit is a bean like pod
  tree often looks blighted as a result of locust leaf miner

Honeylocust *(Gleditsia triacanthos)*

  leaves are <u>twice compound</u> (leaflets have leaflets)
  bark & branches have long, sharp-pointed, <u>multiple thorns</u>
  fruit a long twisted bean pod with <u>sweet pulp</u>
  native mostly to Piedmont, but not abundant

One leaf

Black walnut *(Juglans nigra)*

15 to 23 leaflets, leaflets are not sickle shaped
terminal leaflet (the one on the leaf end) often absent
fruit a round green husk containing a ridged black nut shell
bark is ridged and black
formerly widely planted for its nuts

Boxelder maple *(Acer negundo)*

has opposite leaves like other maples
abundant along streams in young forests
only native maple with compound leaves
leaflets usually occur in threes, reminiscent of poison ivy

Green Ash *(Fraxinus pennsylvanica)*

      the only ash abundant below the Mountains

      has <u>both opposite and compound leaves</u>

      <u>bark is soft and spongy</u>. A fingernail can dent it.

      Axillary bud is <u>on top</u> of leaf scar

      axillary bud is the bud located where the leaf attaches

      wing extends about half way up seed body

White Ash *(Fraxinus americana)*

      replaces green ash in Mountains

      grows in rich mountain coves between 2500' and 4000'

      axillary bud is at least <u>partially enveloped</u> by leaf scar.

      wing begins at the end of the seed

leaf scar
& bud

Keith Kanoti, MFS

Mountain Ash *(Sorbus americana)*

NOT related to green ash and white ash
has <u>alternate</u>, compound leaves
found only in Mountains above 5000 feet elevation
diagnostic tree of the spruce-fir forest

Sumac *(Rhus spp.)*

leaves alternate, compound, leaflets toothed
a native **shrub** instead of a tree, but abundant in open areas
usually found in clumps due to multiple root sprouts
fruit a cluster of fuzzy red berries with a tart taste

One Leaf

CHAPTER 4. TREES WITH OPPOSITE LEAVES

"MADogs with Beards and Buckeyed Cats named Paul"

Maple, Ash, Dogwood, Old Mans Beard, Buckeye, Catalpa and Paulownia

All maples have opposite leaves and gray bark that is smooth or flaky. The tiny red to brownish flowers mature into double winged seeds in spring.

Red Maple *(Acer rubrum)*
> by far the most common maple in America
> leaves have <u>teeth</u> as well as <u>shallow lobes</u>.
> Leaf shape is variable depending on genetics and habitat
> leaf undersides are <u>not</u> whitish like silver maple

Jerry Payne, USFS

Silver Maple *(Acer saccharinum)*

not abundant in the South.
leaves have teeth as well as <u>long lobes with deep indentions</u>
leaf undersides are <u>whitish or silvery</u>

Franklin Bonner

Sugar Maple *(Acer saccharum)*

leaves are shaped like the <u>flag of Canada</u>
leaves are lobed, <u>toothless and hairless bleow.</u>
<u>leaves not whitish below</u> like Southern sugar maple
Bark often <u>black</u> with sap dripping from <u>woodpecker holes</u>.

No fuzz below

Southern Sugar Maple (Florida maple) *(Acer floridanum)*

grows along streams in Piedmont and upper Coastal Plain

looks like a small version of sugar maple

grows below the forest canopy as an understory tree.

leaves are **whitish** and **slightly** fuzzy below

usually grows as a single stem

Whitish underside

Chalk maple *(Acer leucoderme)*

understory tree like Southern sugar maple

closely resembles it.

Leaf **greenish, not whitish** below, but is **slightly** fuzzy

often grows as multiple stems

bark often looks chalky white

Striped Maple *(Acer pensylvanicum)*

grows only in Mountains above 2000'
understory tree and sometimes subcanopy
leaves three-lobed, shaped like goose feet
young trunks and branches have distinctive stripes
fruit stalks point down

Mountain Maple *(Acer spicatum)*

grows only in the mountains above 4500'
usually an understory tree
.   leaves have five lobes instead of three.
lacks the stripes of striped maple.
fruit stalks always point up toward the mountains

Boxelder Maple, page 14

Norway Maple (Acer platanoides), is an introduced exotic maple
with leaves about as wide as they are long.

Ash, page 15

Flowering Dogwood _Cornus florida)_

     small understory tree
     widely planted as an ornamental tree
     leaf <u>veins run roughly parallel</u> to each other
     <u>large white four-petaled flowers</u>
     red berry-like drupe
     mature bark breaks into dark square plates (<u>alligator bark</u>)

The wood of the flowering dogwod tree is among the hardest in
North America. Pioneers made wooden wedges called gluts of
dogwood to help in splitting logs. The hardness of the wood and
its tendency to get smoother with use made it highly desirable for
textile mill shuttles, machinery bearings and spools during the
water-powered days of America's textile industry.

Swamp Dogwood *(Cornus stricta)*

   leaves look like those of flowering dogwood
   small white flowers in clusters
   fruit blue, instead of red
   prefers swamps and stream bottoms
   not abundant

Alternate-leaf dogwood *(Cornus alternifolia)*

   leaves alternate instead of opposite!
   more abundant in the Mountains than the Piedmont
   young trunks and branches distinctive greenish color
   small white flowers in clusters
   fruit dark blue, berry-like drupe

Fringetree (Old-mans-beard) *(Chionanthus virginicus)*

fairly rare understory tree
white, strap-like flowers look like an old man's beard
grows on rich sites along streams

Painted Buckeye *(Aesculus sylvatica)*

leaves are palmate (leaflets radiate from a palm-like center)
small <u>shrub-like understory tree</u>
<u>native mainly to the Piedmont</u>
prefers mature oak-hickory forests
<u>creamy yellow flowers and</u> fruit a "buckeye"

Red Buckeye *(Aesculus pavia)*

leaves are palmate (leaflets radiate from a palm-like center)
grows mostly in the <u>Coastal Plain,</u> but planted elsewhere
usually grows taller than painted buckeye
has <u>red flowers</u> that attract hummingbirds, & buckeye fruit

Yellow Buckeye *(Aesculus octandra)*

> leaves are palmate (leaflets radiate from a palm-like center)
> large forest <u>canopy tree</u>,
> restricted to the <u>Mountains</u>
> yellow flowers
> <u>very stout twigs</u>
> flaky <u>"puzzle piece" bark</u>
> fruit a "buckeye"

Mature Buckeye

Immature

The fruit of the buckeye (a buckeye) was named for its obvious resemblance to the eye of a deer. The American Indians were the first to name it, calling it hetuck, which meant buckeye in their language. Though buckeye fruit contains a poison called glycoside, the Indians used heat and leaching to remove it and ate them.

Don't be tempted to try this, as the Indians also used crushed buckeyes thrown into rivers and lakes to poison fish. Cooking supposedly removed the poison, rendering the fish edible. Somehow the buckeye came to symbolize good luck, and old timers carried a lucky buckeye with them, passing it down the generations.

Southern Catalpa *(Catalpa bignonioides)*

large toothless, heart-shaped leaves
fairly rare, medium sized tree of river banks and swamps
produces large white flowers
seed pods very long narrow, look like long skinny cigars
catalpa worm regularly defoliates this tree in summer

Royal Paulownia *(Paulownia tomentosa)*

introduced exotic from Asia
large toothless, heart-shaped leaves are fuzzy
large pink to blue flowers
black oval mature seed pods with white cottony seeds.

CHAPTER 5. TREES WITH SIMPLE, ALTERNATE TOOTHLESS LEAVES

"My toothless Pawpaw found a Magic Red Cucumber in Miss Simmons purse that gave him Blackgums."

Pawpaw, Magnolias, Red Bay, Redbud, Cucumbertree, Persimmon, Blackgum

Pawpaw (*Asimina triloba*) and (*Asimina parviflora*)
     multiple-stemmed understory shrub to 12 feet tall
     grows in clonal colonies
     crushed leaves smell like bell pepper
     twig end buds brown and fuzzy
     flowers small, red, leathery
     fruit 4-inch yellowish berry, rarely develops to maturity

Wendy VanDyk Evans

Brian Lockhart

The "bell pepper" smell of pawpaw leaves comes from acetogenin a chemical the plant uses to repel insects. Only zebra swallowtail butterfly larvae successfully feed on them. Pawpaw seeds contain chemicals potentially useful in fighting prostate and colon cancer.

Southern Magnolia (*Magnolia grandiflora*)

- leaves evergreen, leathery, glossy above, brownish below
- flowers very large, white and lemony fragrant
- mature fruit a cone containing bright red berries
- widely planted as an ornamental
- has <u>stipular rings</u> (ring around the stem where leaf attaches)

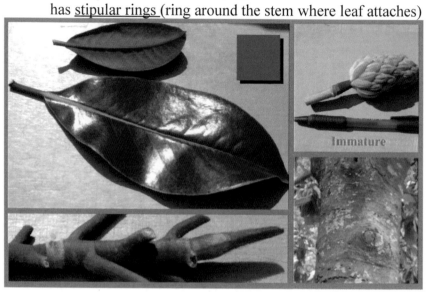

Sweetbay Magnolia (*Magnolia virginiana*)

- native to Coastal Plain, but widely planted elsewhere
- leaves evergreen, <u>whitish beneath</u>
- flower and fruit like southern magnolia but smaller
- has <u>stipular rings</u> (ring around the stem where leaf attaches)

Bigleaf Magnolia (*Magnolia macrophylla*)

       leaves <u>deciduous,</u> with <u>ear-shaped bases</u> , & <u>very large</u>

       usually a subcanopy or understory tree

       found mostly in Piedmont

       has stipular rings (ring around the stem where leaf attaches)

Fraser Magnolia (*Magnolia fraseri*)

       leaves <u>deciduous with ear-shaped bases</u>

       most common in middle elevations in <u>Mountains</u>

       often grows as a multiple trunk

       usually a subcanopy or canopy tree

       has <u>stipular rings</u> (ring around the stem where leaf attaches)

Umbrella Magnolia *(Magnolia tripetala)*
leaves deciduous, <u>without ear-shaped base & large</u>
leaves arranged in <u>whorls</u>, reminiscent of an umbrella
most common in low elevation Mountains
has stipular rings (ring around the stem where leaf attaches)

Cucumbertree *(Magnolia acuminata)*
leaves deciduous, <u>without ear-shaped base</u>
most abundant in mountains, but also occurs in Piedmont
mature fruit a cone with bright red berries
prefers low and middle elevation mountain coves
has stipular rings (ring around the stem where leaf attaches)

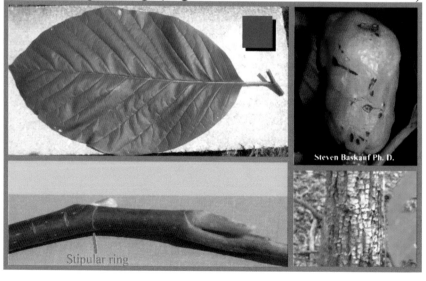

Red Bay (*Persea borbonia*)

    crushed leaves are <u>fragrant</u>

    leaves often have <u>insect galls (dark spot in photo)</u>

    twigs and buds fuzzy

    native to coastal plain, but planted elsewhere

Franklin Bonner, USFS

Eastern redbud (*Cercis canadensis*)

    leaves are <u>heart shaped</u>

    flower, <u>red to purple</u> blooms in early spring with dogwood

    fruit a short bean pod

    small understory tree

    <u>widely planted as an ornamental</u>

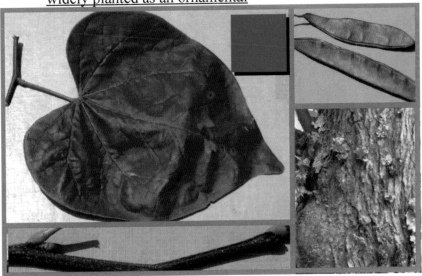

Persimmon *(Diospyros virginiana)*
    canopy tree
    leaves eye shaped, often with <u>distinctive black dots</u>
    bark black and breaking into <u>square blocks</u>
    fruit a <u>persimmon</u>

Blackgum *(Nyssa sylvatica)*
    canopy tree
    leaves tear shaped (ovate), or eye-shaped (elliptical)
    leaf ends sometimes have <u>horn-like points</u> (as in photo)
    twigs smooth and <u>tan colored</u>
    limbs often emerge from trunk as <u>90 degree angle</u>

CHAPTER 6. TREES WITH SIMPLE, ALTERNATE TOOTHED LEAVES

"Elmer is the son of a Birch who Hacked the Horn off a Buck with a Silver Service sword."

Elms, **B**irches, **H**ackberrys, **H**ornbeams, **B**uckthorn, **S**ilverbell, **S**erviceberry

"Willy and Al Hollered and drank Sour Cherry wine when they caught a Cottonpickin' Bass at the Beach."

Willow, **A**lder, **H**olly, **S**ourwood, **C**herry, **C**ottonwood, **B**asswood, **B**eech

Winged Elm *(Ulmus alata)*

   leaves small, smooth on top and bottom
   leaf bases usually even (ie, not uneven)
   twigs often have <u>corky wings</u>
   often found in subcanopy
   considered a weedy tree

Franklin Bonner, USFS

American Elm *(Ulmus americana)*

> Canopy tree
> Leaves medium, <u>usually smooth above and below</u>
> leaf bases usually <u>very uneven</u>
> not abundant since the Dutch elm disease attacked

Slippery Elm (Red Elm) *(Ulmus rubra)*

> canopy tree
> usually found along streams, but not abundant
> leaves <u>very rough on upper surface</u>
> leaves bases often <u>but not always</u> uneven

River Birch *(Betula nigra)*

bark peels into <u>thin pinkish strips</u>
grows along large streams, but widely planted elsewhere
native to Piedmont and upper Coastal Plain
rarely found in Mountains, and never above 2500'

Yellow Birch *(Betula alleghaniensis)*

bark peels into thin <u>silvery or golden strips</u>
crushed twigs smell and taste like <u>wintergreen</u>
restricted to the <u>Mountains above 3000'</u>
leaves often double-toothed
twigs are <u>greenish gray</u>

Black Birch *(Betula lenta)*

      mature bark is gray with black vertical cracks; does not peel
      leaves mostly singly toothed, rarely doubly toothed
      twigs are dark shiny red & have wintergreen taste and odor
      restricted to the Mountains above 1500'
      leaves are two ranked, falsely appearing opposite

Richard Webb

Horace Kephart says birch wood makes some of the best fuel available, igniting quickly and burning long, hot with good coals. Yellow birch burns even better green than dried, says he. Both trees contain wintergreen oil, a flammable substance. In the past, wintergreen oil was extracted from black birch, especially, and used to flavor medicines and candy.

Hackberry *(Celtis occidentalis)*

native to Cumberland Plateau and Ridge and Valley
fairly rare in Piedmont, absent in the Coastal Plain
leaves rough, often with toothless and uneven bases
mature bark has " warts"
mature fruit a purple berry-like drupe

Georgia Hackberry *(Celtis tenuifolia)*

abundant only in Piedmont province
small tree, seldom taller than 25'
leaves and bark similar to hackberry
mature fruit orange
round twig galls are usually present and diagnostic

Sugarberry *(Celtis laevigata)*

mature bark has <u>warts</u>
leaves shiny and smooth with few teeth, especially at base
<u>leaf tips long, narrow and pointed</u>
mature fruit orange
grows along streams

Franklin Bonner, USFS

American Hornbeam *(Carpinus caroliniana)*
      bark smooth, gray with <u>muscular bulges</u>
      small understory tree along streams
      leaf bases not uneven
      leaves <u>hairless below</u>
      mature fruit looks like "<u>praying hands</u>"

Eastern Hophornbeam *(Ostrya virginiana)*
      <u>bark is flaky</u> with narrow scales *bugs "hop" over the scales*
      leaves are <u>hairy below</u>
      mature fruit looks like large <u>oat or hop seeds</u>
      fruit has hairs that sting and itch when touched
      understory to subcanopy tree

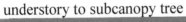

Carolina Buckthorn *(Rhamnus caroliniana)*

        small, <u>fairly rare</u> understory tree
        leaves shiny with conspicuous veins
        immature fruit green, then bright red
        mature fruit black and berry-like

Blue When Ripe

Bill Cook MSU

Carolina Silverbell *(Halesia carolina)*

        bark on young stems and trunks has <u>conspicuous stripes</u>
        understory tree along rivers and large streams
        leaf teeth are rather small
        flowers white and bell-shaped

Chris Evans, RTR

Young Bark   Mature Bark

Downy Serviceberry *(Amelanchier arborea)*
- leaves have <u>heart-shaped bases</u>
- mature bark is black with distinctive <u>dark vertical slits</u>
- small understory tree
- white flowers appear <u>before leaves in early spring</u>
- mature fruit an edible red to purple berry

Allegheny Serviceberry *(Amelancier laevis)*
- found only in <u>Mountains</u> above 2000 feet elevation
- leaves have long tapered tips
- flowers emerge <u>after the leaves</u>

"Willy and Al Hollered and drank Sour Cherry wine when they caught a Cottonpickin' Bass at the Beach."

Willow, Alder, Holly, Sourwood, Cherry, Cottonwood, Basswood, Beech

Black Willow *(Salix nigra)*
  leaves long and narrow
   always grows in sunny areas near water

Paul Wray, ISU

Hazel Alder *(Alnus serrulata)*

always grows <u>near water</u>
<u>brown cones from last year are often on the tree</u>
small shrubby tree

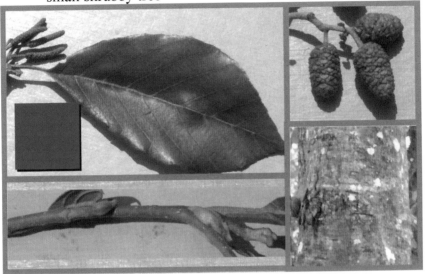

American Holly *(Ilex opaca)*

evergreen subcanopy tree
leaves thick and shiny with <u>sharp "holly" spines</u>
bark smooth and dark gray

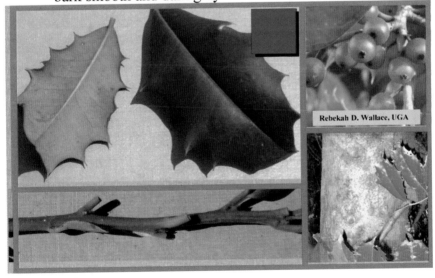

Mountain Holly *(Ilex montana)*

deciduous (leaves drop in autumn) understory tree
grows only at high elevations in the Mountains
leaf veins appear sunken below leaf surface
leaves look slightly wrinkled
red berry often remains into winter

Mature Berries RED

Yaupon Holly *(Ilex vomitoria)*

evergreen understory tree
native to Coastal Plain, but often planted as ornamental
leaves small, thick and shiny with a few big teeth
leaves don't have spines

Mature Berries RED

Sourwood *(Oxydendrum arboreum)*

leaves long and narrow with <u>tiny teeth</u>
crushed leaves taste sour
mature bark reddish with flat-topped, "topographic"ridges
subcanopy tree with crooked, <u>zig-zag growth pattern</u>
<u>flower stalks look like gracfully posed hand</u>

Black Cherry *(Prunus serotina)*

crushed leaves smell like <u>bitter almond</u>
bark on young stems <u>reddish to gray and shiny</u>
fruit a wild black cherry
canopy or subcanopy tree
<u>black knot fungus causes a large black trunk canker</u>

Carolina Laurelcherry *(Prunus caroliniana)*
thick shiny evergreen leaves
crushed leaves smell like vanilla
dark blue berries
native to Coastal Plain, but planted elsewhere

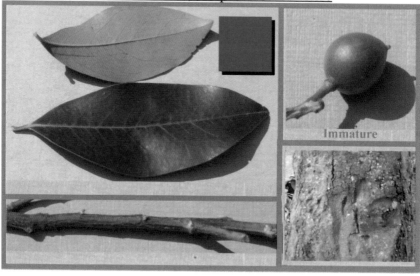

Immature

Pin Cherry(Fire Cherry *(Prunus pensylvanica)*
only found in high elevation Mountains
bark fiery bronze color
leaves with long narrow points
flowers much larger than black cherry

Dave Powell, USDA

Eastern Cottonwood *(Populus deltoides)*

uncommon
triangular-shaped leaves
leaves wave and "tremble" in the wind
grows along streams

White Basswood *(Tilia heterophylla)*

heart-shaped leaves often with <u>uneven bases</u>
fruit structure very unique with <u>large leafy bract</u>
grows mostly in Mountains along streams
old trees often surrounded by a <u>ring of sprouts</u>

American Beech *(Fagus grandifolia)*

bark <u>smooth and gray, often with initials</u> carved in it
leaves have a <u>papery feel</u>, leaf veins are conspicuous
twig end buds are long, round and pointed <u>like tiny cigars</u>
leaves usually stay on tree <u>through winter</u>
mature fruit a three-angle nut inside a bur-like capsule

American Chestnut *(Castanea dentata)*

once abundant in upper Piedmont and Mountains
mature trees wiped out by chestnut blight by 1950
found in Mountains as multi-stemmed sprouts
leaf teeth are big and jagged

48

CHAPTER 7. TREES WITH LOBED LEAVES

"Sweet Mable, the Sassy and Popular Mulberry, got Sick in Oklahoma."

Sweetgum, Maple, Sassafras, Poplar, **Mulberry**, Sycamore, Oaks

Sweetgum (Liquidambar styraciflua)
> star shaped leaves
> sweetgum balls often remain on tree in winter
> leaves are <u>alternate</u> instead of opposite like maples

Maple page 17

Sassafras *(Sassafras albidum)*

      leaf shape can be <u>3-lobed, mitten-shaped or unlobed</u>

      leaves toothless

      twig end greenish

      bark brownish red and fibrous looking

      roots smell like <u>sassafras tea</u>

Yellow Poplar (Tulip Poplar)*(Liriodendron tulipifera)*

      leaf shaped like a <u>tulip or a cat's head</u>

      twig has <u>stipular rings</u>

      fruit a clump of winged seeds like a mini chandelier

      trunk cylindrical and straight

50

Red Mulberry *(Morus rubra)*

      leaf shape can be 3-lobed, mitten-shaped or unlobed
      leaves have teeth
      leaf underside <u>hairy</u>
      small understory tree found throughout
      fruit a red or dark blue mulberry
      trunk often has flaky swellings

White Mulberry *(Morus alba)*

      leaf shape can be 3-lobed, mitten-shaped or unlobed
      leaves <u>shiny and hairless</u>
      <u>very rare compared to red mulberry</u>

Paul Resslar, VWC

American Sycamore *(Platanus occidentalis)*

    always grows near streams
    upper trunk is <u>stark white</u> and looks dead
    lower trunk is flaky brown

Oaks are a large group of trees that are fairly easy to identify as a group. Look for the **multiple buds on the twig ends,** a consistent oak characteristic. Also look for acorns in the tree or on the ground below. Mature oaks are usually large canopy trees, dominating the forest.

There are two major groups of oaks:

White Oak Group
> leaf lobes are rounded
> leaf lobes lack small spines called bristles on the lobe ends
> bark is usually dark gray or light gray

The white oak group includes:
> White Oak
> Post Oak
> Chestnut Oak
> Overcup Oak
> Live Oak

Red Oak Group
> leaf lobes are pointed
> leaf lobes are bristle tipped, though it's not always obvious
> bark is usually dark gray or black

The red oak group includes:
> Northern Red Oak
> Scarlet Oak
> Southern Red Oak
> Bluejack Oak
> Turkey Oak
> Laurel Oak
> Blackjack Oak
> Black Oak
> Water Oak
> Willow Oak

White Oak *(Quercus alba)*

      white oak group
      mature bark light gray <u>often with big gray flakes</u>
      leaves with rounded lobes lacking bristles
      acorn shaped like a bullet

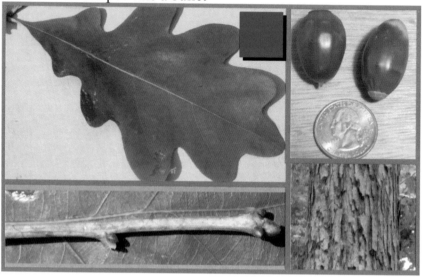

Post Oak *(Quercus sellata)*

      white oak group
      leaves <u>fairly thick, forming a rough cross shape</u>
      bark light gray, but does not have flakes like white oak
      often found growing on dry ridgetops
      acorns not distinctive

Paul Wray, ISU

Chestnut Oak *(Quercus prinus)*

     white oak group
     leaf lobes small, forming a <u>scalloped leaf edge</u>
     mature bark breaking into <u>long flat topped ridges</u>
     <u>acorns very large</u> compared to other oaks
     most abundant in the Mountains and upper Piedmont

Overcup Oak *(Quercus lyrata)*

     found along Piedmont rivers and swamps
     fairly rare in the wild, but planted as an ornamental
     lower leaf indentions are often "squared off"
     <u>acorn cap completely encloses mature acorn</u>

Live Oak *(Quercus virginiana)*
> white oak group
> leaves evergreen and leathery
> native to Coastal Plain, but planted elsewhere
> acorns round and black

Franklin Bonner

Swamp Chestnut Oak *(Quercus michauxii)* not pictured here has scalloped leaves like chestnut oak and flaky light gray bark like white oak. It's acorns are large like chestnut oak. It is most abundant on bottomlands in the lower Piedmont and Coastal Plain provinces of the South.

Northern Red Oak *(Quercus rubra)*

  red oak group
  bark with wide gray stripes <u>"ski trails"</u>
  leaves big and wide with wide lobes, <u>"bear paw shape"</u>
  leaves, twig and buds are <u>hairless</u>
  acorn is barrel shaped

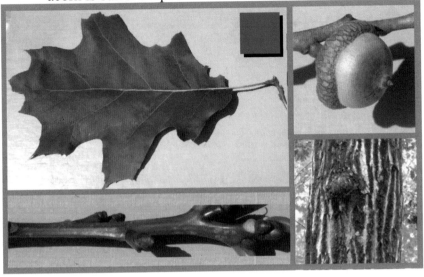

Scarlet Oak *(Quercus coccinea)*

  red oak group
  leaves with <u>narrow lobes separated by deep indentions</u>
  bark often has narrow gray stripes
  lower trunk often has dead limbs
  acorn has <u>concentric rings around acorn tip</u>

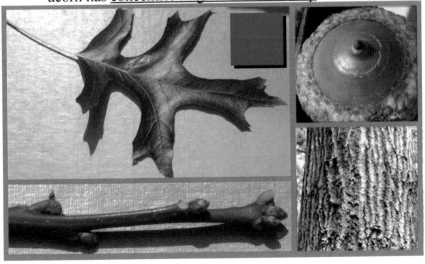

Southern Red Oak *(Quercus falcata)*

     red oak group
     leaves can have a variety of shapes, but
     lobes on leaf ends <u>often have a bell shape</u>
     mature bark is black and ridged

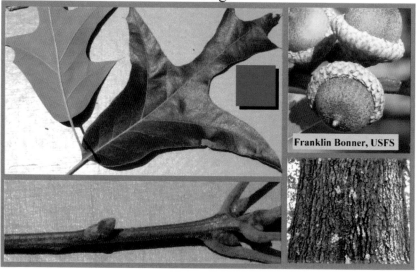

Franklin Bonner, USFS

Bluejack Oak *(Quercus incana)*

     sandy ridges in the Coastal Plain
     always a small shrub-like tree
     <u>leaf underside is bluish or whitish</u>
     twigs and buds are slender

Catnapin.com

Turkey Oak *(Quercus laevis)*

grows exclusively in Coastal Plain
found on sandy ridgetops, often with longleaf pine
<u>leaves shaped like a turkey foot</u>
<u>leaf stems are twisted</u>
leaves have yellowish veins

Laurel Oak *(Quercus laurifolia)*

leaves shiny green above, paler below
leaves often have partial lobes like photo
grows along streams in the Coastal Plain
leaves usually stay on tree in winter

Blackjack Oak *(Quercus marilandica)*

    usually found on the driest most sterile ridgetops
    leaves very stiff and leathery
    leaves usually 3-lobed and fuzzy below along veins
    bark forms rectangular black plates

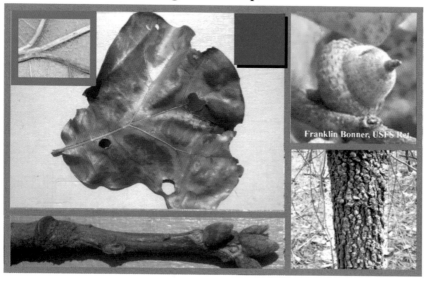

Franklin Bonner, USFS Ret.

Black Oak *(Quercus velutina)*

    red oak group
    lower canopy leaves large and wide (<u>bear paw</u>)
    <u>leaf lower surface and twigs are fuzzy</u>
    upper canopy leaves with deeper indentions
    mature bark black and ridged

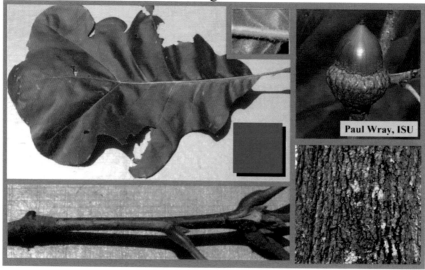

Paul Wray, ISU

Water Oak *(Quercus nigra)*

  red oak group
  leaves often of <u>several shapes</u>, but
  mostly <u>spatula shaped</u>, wider at the end than at the base
  mature bark dark gray to black lacking rough ridges
  acorn small and round

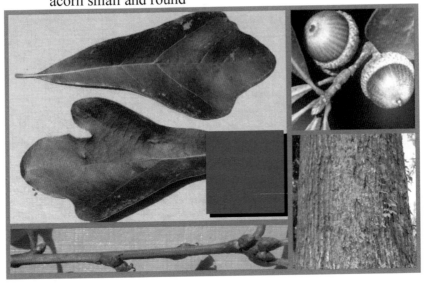

Willow Oak *(Quercus phellos)*

  red oak group
  leaves <u>long and very narrow like willow leaves</u>
  <u>leaf shape does not vary</u> like in water oak
  mature bark dark gray to black lacking rough ridges
  native along streams, but planted elsewhere

Franklin Bonner, USFS

CHAPTER 8. PINES AND OTHER CONIFERS

Pines with 5 needles per bundle:

only white pine

Pines with 2 and 3 needles per bundle:

slash pine and shortleaf pine have mostly 2 needles per bundle, and occasionally 3 needles per bundle

Pines with 3 needles per bundle:

"Lob a Long Pitch into the Pond."

Loblolly, Longleaf, Pitch, Pond

Pines with 2 needles per bundle:

"Virginia will Spruce up the Table Shortly."

Virginia, Spruce, Table-mountain, Shortleaf

White Pine *(Pinus strobus)*
   leaves have <u>5 needles per bundle</u>
   branches <u>arranged in whorls</u> on trunk
   cones lack prickles and are often resin coated
   native to Mountains, but widely planted elsewhere

Slash Pine *(Pinus elliottii)*
   leaves have <u>2 and 3 needles per bundle</u>
   needles are long, but not as long as longleaf pine
   <u>bark is reddish</u>
   <u>cones are reddish with shiny (but not sharp) cone scales</u>
   Coastal Plain native, rarely found elsewhere

Loblolly Pine *(Pinus taeda)*

leaves have <u>3 needles per bundle</u>
needles are medium length (about 6 ")
cones have <u>very sharp prickles</u>

Longleaf Pine *(Pinus palustris)*

<u>leaves long</u>, 3 needles per bundle
<u>cones are very large</u> compared to other pines
twig end buds are long and white
young seedlings look like bunch grass
native to Coastal Plain, but planted elsewhere

Pitch Pine *(Pinus rigida)*
leaves have <u>3 needles per bundle</u>
needles are medium length, usually <u>stiff and twisted</u>
<u>cones are egg shaped</u> with very short or absent stalks
native to dry <u>mountain ridgetops</u>, rare elsewhere

Pond Pine *(Pinus serotina)*
leaves have <u>3 needles per bundle</u>
<u>needles often emerge directly from trunk</u>
<u>cones egg shaped</u>
native to Coastal Plain, but fairly rare there

Virginia Pine *(Pinus virginiana)*

leaves have <u>2 needles per bundle</u>
needles are short
cones are short with distinctive <u>purple lip on cone scales</u>
bark is <u>reddish and scaly</u> with many dead limbs on trunk
Mountains and upper Piedmont on dry ridgetops

Purple cone lip

Spruce Pine *(Pinus glabra)*

leaves have <u>2 needles per bundle</u>
bark is dark and slightly <u>scaly like spruce bark</u>
only Coastal Plain, but fairly rare there

Table-mountain Pine *(Pinus pungens)*

leaves have <u>2 needles per bundle</u>
cones are <u>large and thick with very stout prickles</u>
Mountains above 3000', but rare even there

Shortleaf Pine *(Pinus echinada)*

leaves have <u>2 (rarely 3) short needles per bundle</u>
bark is pocked with pencil-point size <u>pitch pockets</u>
cones are short and not prickly, and <u>lack purple lips</u>
Piedmont and Mountains, infrequent in Coastal Plain
prefers dry ridgetops

No purple lip

Eastern Redcedar *(Juniperus virginiana)*

     most common non-pine evergreen in the South
     a small tree, usually less than 30' tall
     leaves are tiny green scales closely attached to twigs
     fruit a small dark blue berry
     heart wood is red and aromatic

Dawn Redwood *(Metasequoia glyptostroboides)*

     a <u>deciduous</u> (drops leaves in autumn) conifer
     ornamental from <u>China</u> that looks like baldcypress
     does not produce cypress knees
     leaf twigs have an <u>opposite arrangement</u>

Bald Cypress*(Taxodium distichum)*

a <u>deciduous</u> (drops leaves in autumn)conifer
native to Coastal Plain, but planted elsewhere
found in large swamps like <u>Okefenokee</u>
<u>cypress knees</u> often present on ground nearby
mature trunks widened out at base into buttresses
leaf twigs are <u>alternate</u> on the branches

Immature cones

Pond Cypress (*Taxodium ascendens*)

a deciduous(drops leaves in autumn) conifer
native to Coastal Pain, infrequently planted elsewhere
found mostly in shallow wet spots called slews
leaves long and linear, appearing feathery

Immature

Red Spruce *(Picea rubens)*

- native to the mountains above 5000', but planted elsewhere
- needles are <u>stiff, angled-sided and sharp pointed</u>
- needles arranged all around the twig
- twig end buds are ruby red

Fraser Fir *(Abies fraseri)*

- native to mountains above 6000'
- virtually wiped out by the balsam wooly adelgid
- needles <u>soft, flattened and blunt tipped</u>
- needles <u>rounded at base</u> and lacking an attachment stalk
- needles arranged in rows on the twig
- commercially grown and sold as Christmas trees

All photos, Bill Cook, MSU

Eastern Hemlock *(Tsuga canadensis)*

native to mountains between 1500 and 4500 '
frequently planted as an ornamental elsewhere
currently being destroyed by exotic hemlock wooly adelgid
needles soft, flattened, and blunt tipped
needles have a short attachment stalk, not rounded at base

Alphabetical Index

Made in the USA
Charleston, SC
18 March 2014